LEARN TO DRAW

Phineas and Ferb

Phineas and Ferb created by Dan Povenmire and Jeff "Swampy" Marsh
Illustrated by Greg Guler and Nancy Ulene
Written by Scott Peterson

Learn to Draw Phineas and Ferb based on the series created by Dan Povenmire and Jeff "Swampy" Marsh

1 3 5 7 9 10 8 6 4 2

Table of Contents

There are 104 days of summer vacation, and each of those days is as precious as aglets (you know, those little stoppers at the end of your shoelaces) to stepbrothers Phineas Flynn and Ferb Fletcher. Their goal is to make the most of every day, filling their summer with cool inventions, wild adventures, and—for some reason—giant, floating baby heads.

Phineas Flynn has a way with words and an unlimited imagination. If he can dream it, he can do it. And he usually does. Ferb Fletcher is more a man of action, letting his deeds speak for him…but when he does speak, it's worth listening to. Together they have created some of the greatest spectacles their hometown of Danville has ever seen…but their mother has not.

"Ferb, I know what we're gonna do today," Phineas says each morning before they launch into that day's project. Whether it's building the world's biggest roller coaster, a robot rodeo, or a pickle the size of Pluto, there is no limit to what they can do. They've wrangled cattle through a mall, stopped an alien bounty hunter, and even traveled through time. Twice! You might ask, "Aren't they a little young to do all this?" Yes, yes, they are. (The fact that you are asking questions of a book is a bit odd, but we'll ignore that for now.)

But they aren't alone in their quest for the best day ever. Helping them with their fun are their three best friends, Buford Van Stomm, Baljeet Rai, and Isabella Garcia-Shapiro. Buford is known as a big bully, although he saves most of his wedgies for Baljeet. Baljeet is highly intelligent and obsessed with education and grades. Isabella, on the other hand, is the self-assured leader of the Fireside Girls. She splits her time between earning merit patches with her troop and helping Phineas and Ferb. Well, mostly helping Phineas. She has a major crush on him.

Unfortunately, there is one major obstacle to the kids' fun-seeking efforts: the Abominable Snowman! (No, not really.) It's Phineas and Ferb's older sister, Candace Flynn. She thinks the crazy things they do are dangerous, abnormal, and just not right. She believes it's her duty to reveal her brothers' shenanigans to their mother and bust them. And she is more than a little obsessed. Other than her crush, Jeremy Johnson, Candace thinks of nothing but busting Phineas and Ferb 24-7. She often mutters to herself, "They're going down, down, down."

Candace has tried everything in her drive to bust the boys: Gathering evidence. Taking pictures. Even yanking her mom from the shower and carrying her to the backyard to see what the boys are doing. But it never works out for Candace.

Part of the problem is that her mom, Linda Flynn-Fletcher, is a very busy woman. She is raising three kids; supporting her husband, Lawrence Fletcher, at his antique store; running errands; and taking every adult education class offered in Danville. She doesn't have time to drop everything and run home every time Candace calls. By the time Mom does get home, the boys' inventions have somehow disappeared, and Candace is defeated once again.

The one remaining member of the Flynn-Fletcher family is their pet platypus, Perry. This blue-green creature with his webbed feet, duck-like bill, and beaver tail is one of only a few semi-aquatic, egg-laying

mammals on the planet. (For more information, visit your local library!) These creatures are very interesting looking, but they don't do much.

Except that this platypus is also a secret agent. When Perry slaps on his trademark fedora, he becomes a crime-fighter known as Agent P. No one in the family knows about his double life, and when he's off on a mission, they can often be heard asking, "Hey, where's Perry?"

Perry belongs to the OWCA (Organization Without a Cool Acronym). It is filled with animal agents who work to stop evil in the Tri-State Area. Major Monogram is Perry's immediate supervisor. When Perry slips through a secret panel and slides down a tube into his underground lair, it is Major Monogram that's waiting there to give him his assignment: Stop Dr. Doofenshmirtz!

Dr. Heinz Doofenshmirtz is Perry's long-time nemesis. Originally from the small town of Gimmelshtump in the Eastern European nation of Druselstein, Dr. Doofenshmirtz now resides in the penthouse suite of Doofenshmirtz Evil Incorporated in downtown Danville. He lives with a robot named Norm, has a teenage daughter named Vanessa, and is a member of an evil society called L,O,V,E M,U,F,F,I,N. He also loves old cheese, long walks on the beach, and peanut brittle.

Doof's primary focus in life is evil. Each day, Perry breaks in to stop Dr. Doofenshmirtz's latest evil plan and gets trapped in one of Doof's ingenious traps. Doof then takes the time to explain his entire evil plan to take over the Tri-State Area. Not the world—he likes to start with manageable goals. Then he reveals his latest diabolical invention. He calls these inventions "inators" and has built some very unusual ones, including a ballgown-inator, a de-love-inator, an everything-evil-inator, a hot-dog-revenge-inator, and even a monkey-enslav-inator.

In the end, Perry always prevails, stopping the scheme and destroying Doof's inator.

Perry rockets away as Doof yells, "Curse you, Perry the Platypus!"

Strangely enough, Doof and Perry's actions usually intersect with Phineas and Ferb's plans for the day, often taking away whatever they have created before their mom can see it. The boys don't mind because it helps with clean up and besides, they've already had their fun.

So now that you know a little bit about the world of Phineas and Ferb, pick up a pencil and start drawing them. Draw! Draw like the wind, my friend! "Seize the day," as Phineas would say, because summer is short, and it's your job to make the most of it. So stick with us 'cause Phineas and Ferb are gonna do it all!

Tools & Materials

Before you begin drawing, you will need to do what Ferb does and gather the right tools. Start with a regular pencil, an eraser, and a pencil sharpener. When you're finished with your drawing, you can bring your characters to life by adding color with crayons, colored pencils, markers, or even watercolor or acrylic paints!

Getting Started

Professional artists draw characters in steps. The key is to start with simple shapes and gradually add the details. The blue lines will help guide you through the process.

Phineas Flynn

Phineas is the most creative, triangle-headed kid that you'll ever meet. Full of ideas and a sense of adventure, there is nothing he won't try to wring the most fun from his summer.

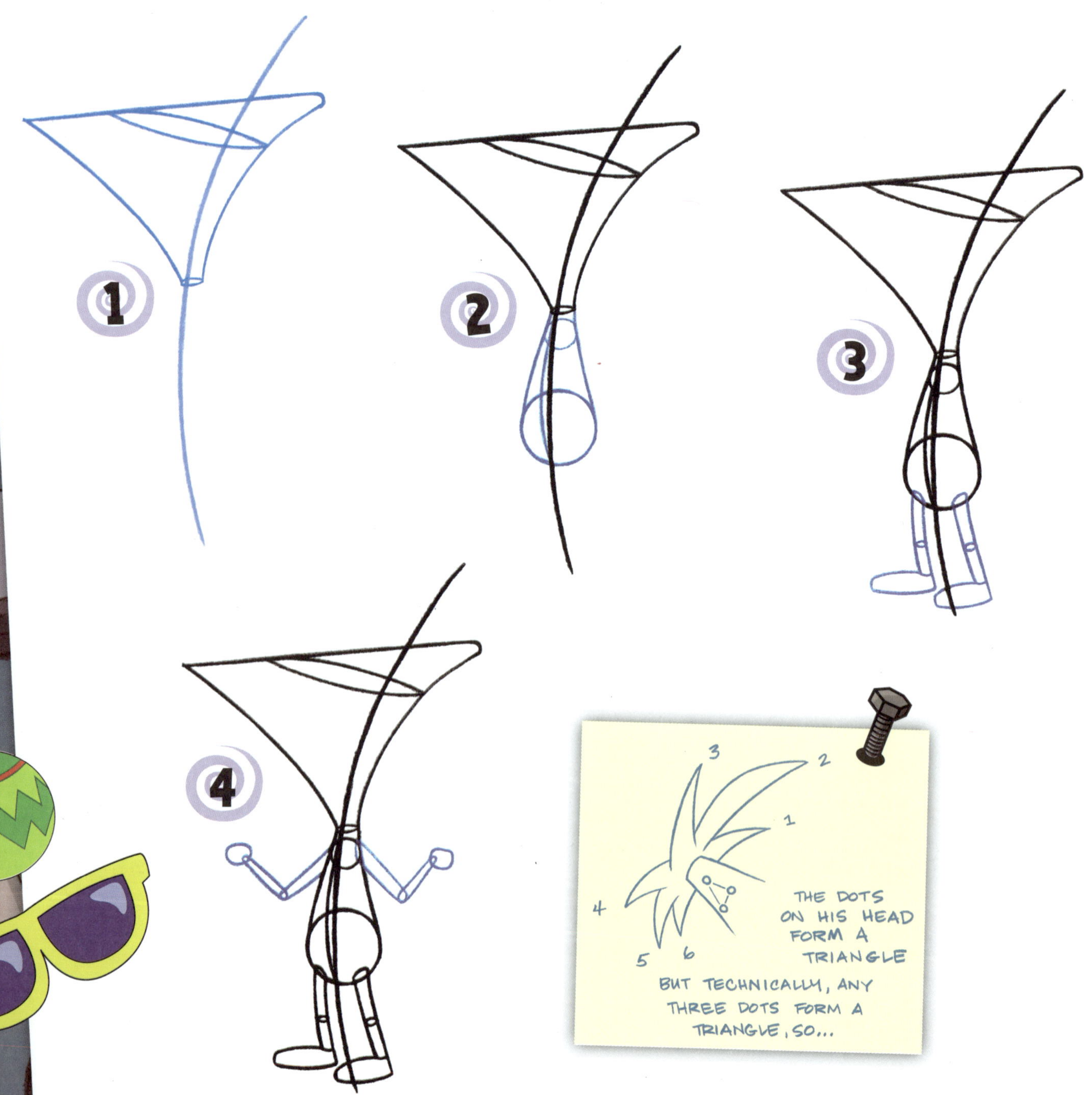

KEEP THE BACK OF HIS HEAD CURVED
PHINEAS HAS A SLIGHT CHIN
5
6
NOTE THAT ALL PHINEAS AND FERB CHARACTERS HAVE A "3" TO INDICATE THE DETAIL OF THE EAR
UNLESS THEY ARE FACING RIGHT, IN WHICH CASE THEY HAVE AN "E" FOR THE EAR
7
8
KEEP A SLIGHT CURVE TO HIS LEG
NO SOCKS... JUST HIGH TOPS
WHO KNEW PHINEAS WAS SUCH A FASHION PLATE?

Ferb Fletcher

Ferb is an inventor extraordinaire, never far from his blueprints and tools. He speaks quietly, but carries a big blowtorch. He is calm in a crisis, and nothing distracts him from the task at hand…except maybe for Vanessa—Dr. Doofenshmirtz's too cool daughter.

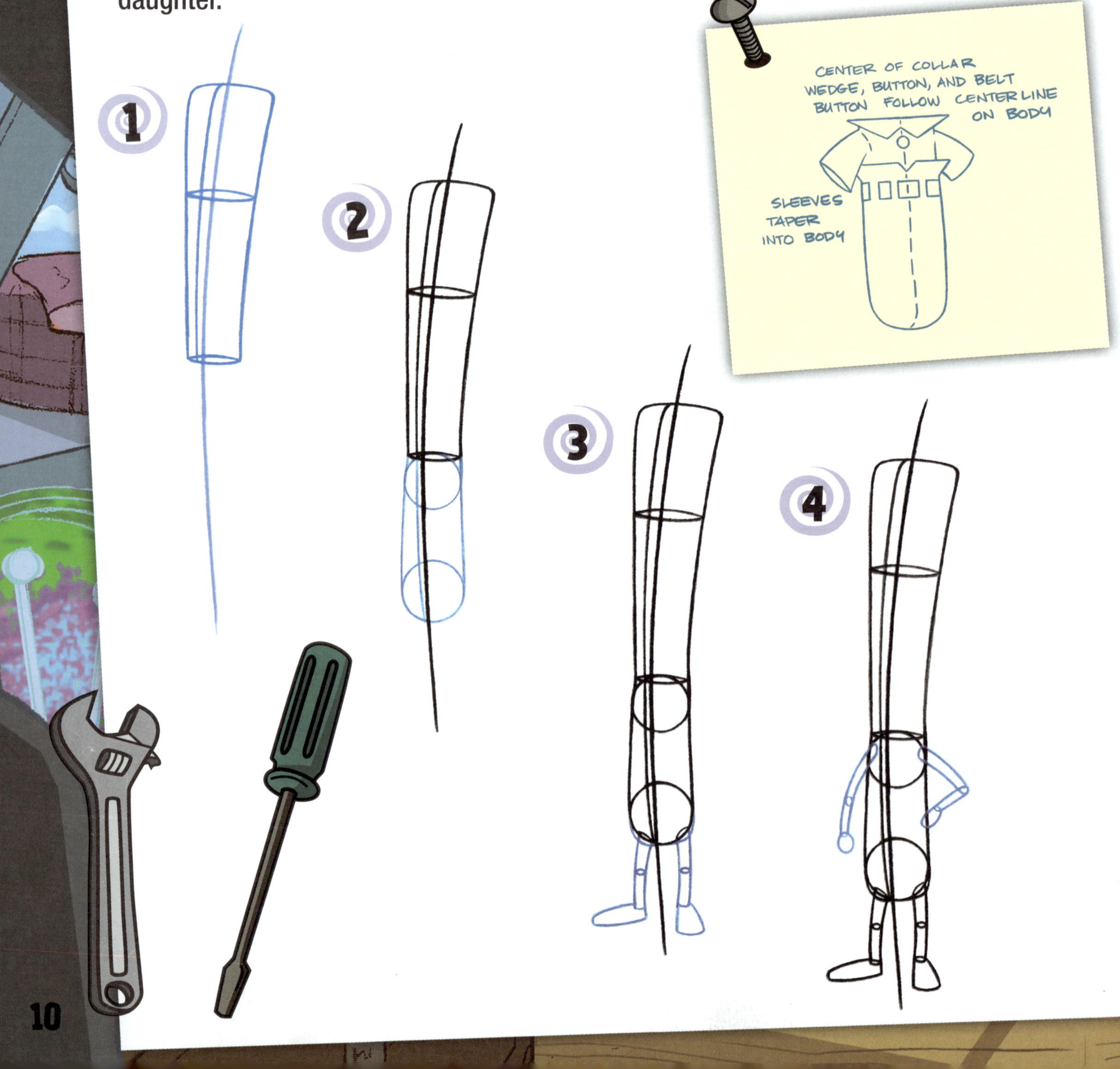

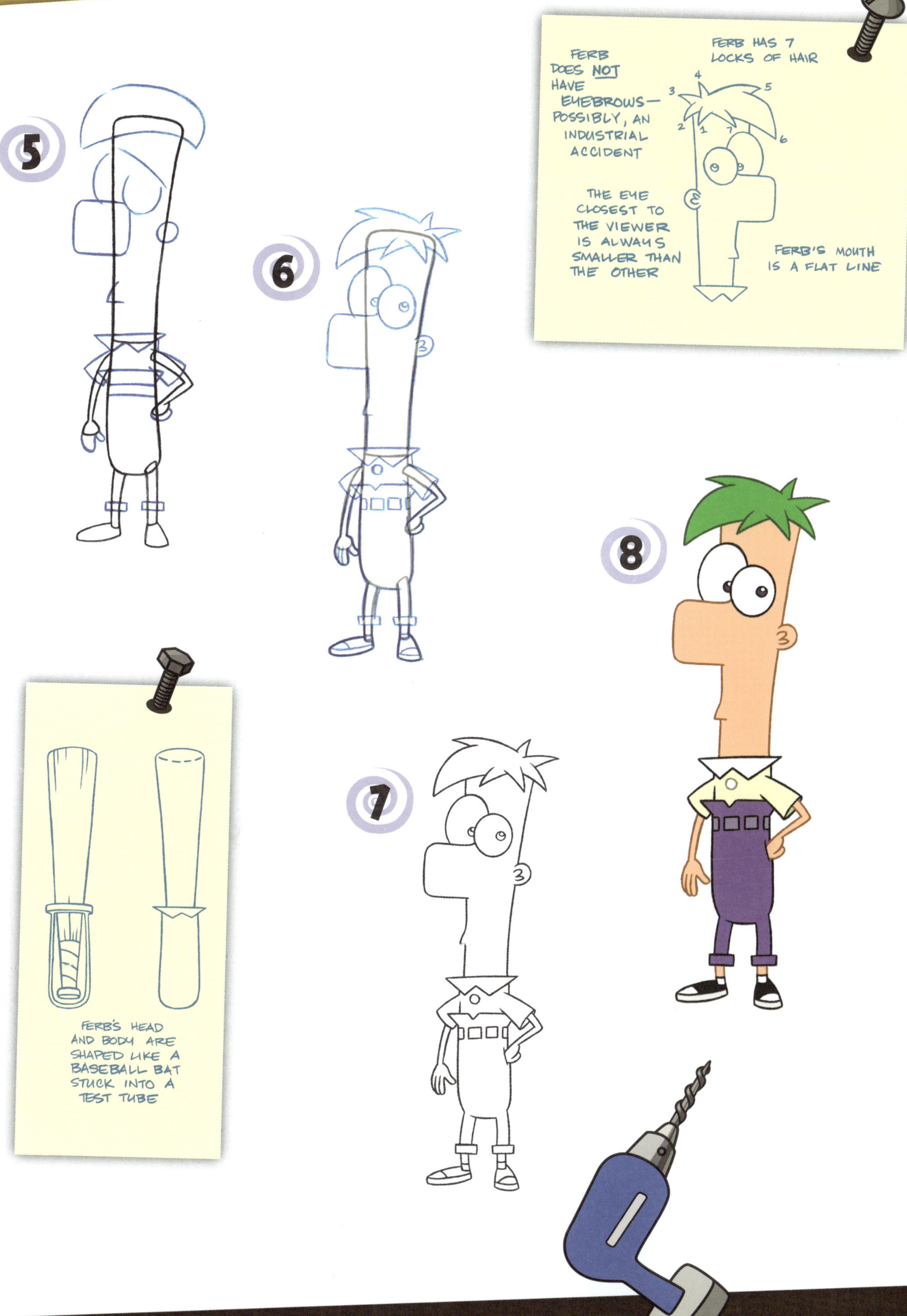
5
6
7
8
FERB DOES NOT HAVE EYEBROWS— POSSIBLY, AN INDUSTRIAL ACCIDENT
FERB HAS 7 LOCKS OF HAIR
THE EYE CLOSEST TO THE VIEWER IS ALWAYS SMALLER THAN THE OTHER
FERB'S MOUTH IS A FLAT LINE
FERB'S HEAD AND BODY ARE SHAPED LIKE A BASEBALL BAT STUCK INTO A TEST TUBE

Candace Flynn

Candace is a high-strung teenager obsessed with busting her brothers. She loves her bros, but she desperately wants to prove to her mom that they are up to something. Sadly, she is her own worst enemy. (Oh, and she has an unusually long neck.)

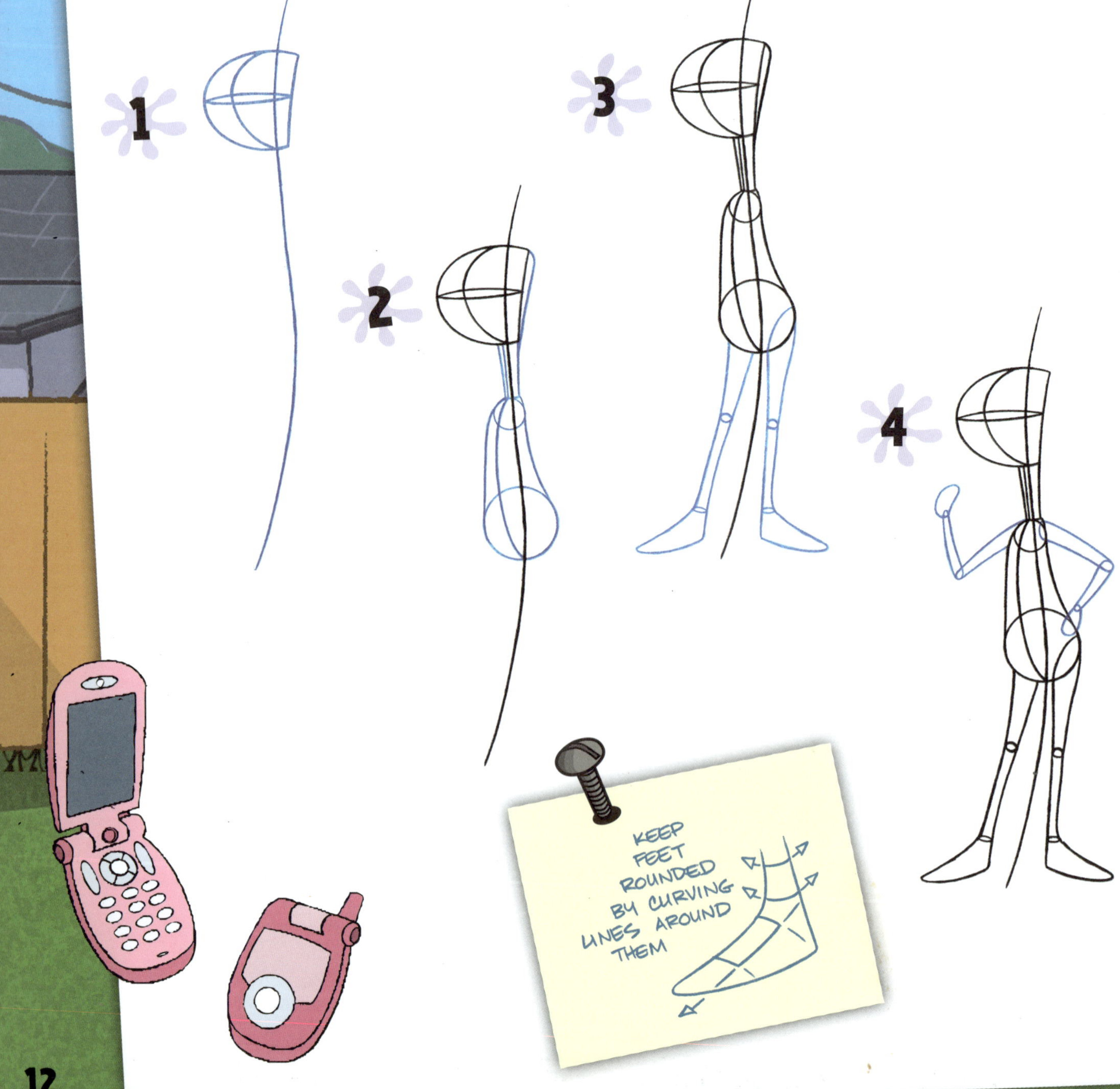

5

6

7

8

HAIR CURVE
WITH HE
NECK
REMEMBER
HER EYELASHES—
AND THE ALAMO

ALWAYS DRAW EYES
AS OVALS AND THEN
REMOVE LIDS

Buford Van Stomm

Buford is the neighborhood bully who has grown into a buddy and become part of Phineas and Ferb's group of friends. He may not be the brightest guy around, but he knows more than you might think. He's a tough cookie (oatmeal raisin to be precise) and is rarely impressed.

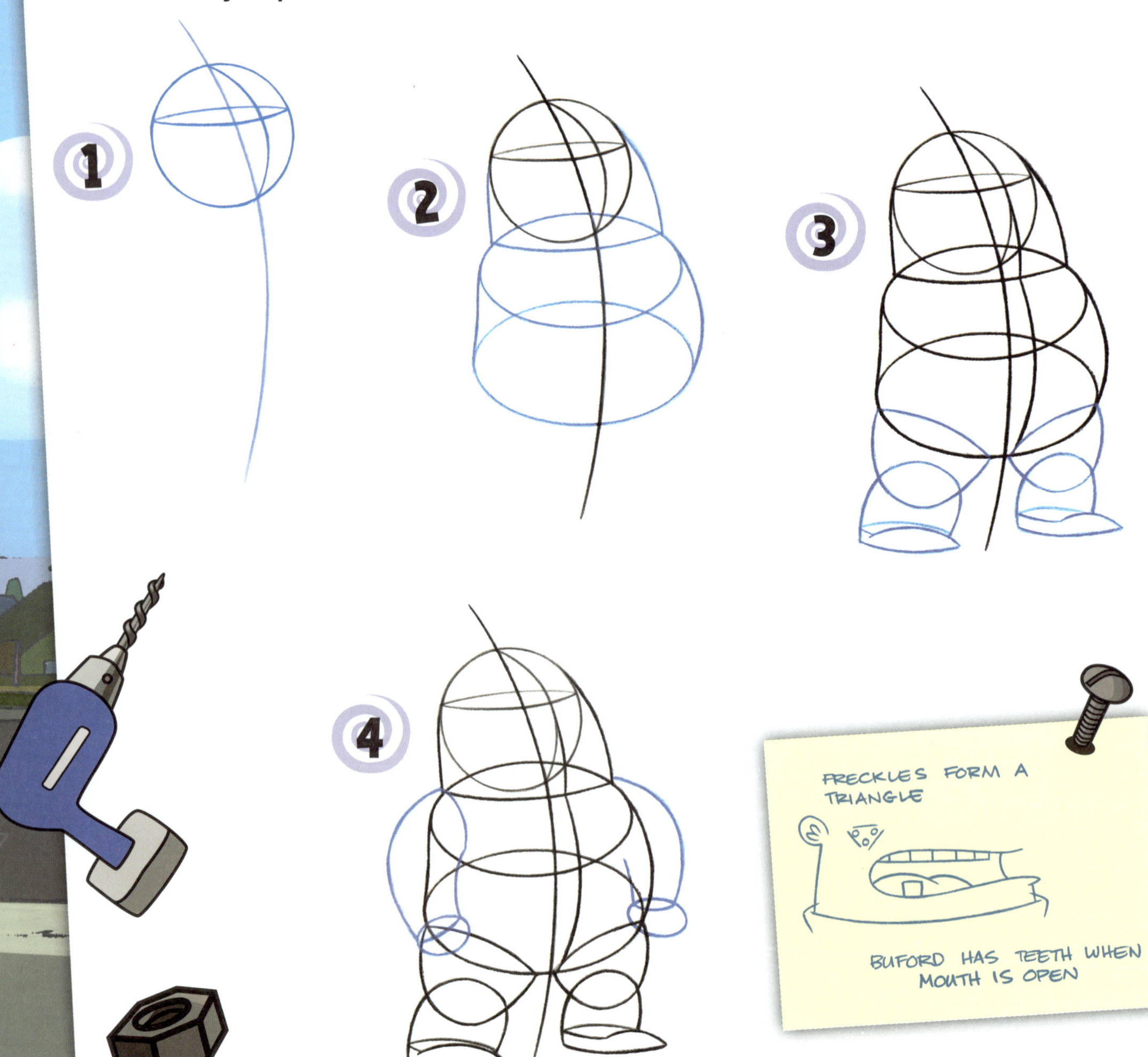

5

BUFORD HAS
TWO NOTCHES IN HIS
HAIR
KEEP HIS
EYES ON
ONE LINE
ONLY ONE TOOTH IS
VISIBLE WHEN HIS
MOUTH IS CLOSED—
HOW DOES THIS GUY CHEW?

6

7

8

TAPER
SLEEVES
UP TO
SHOULDERS

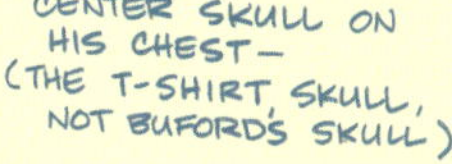
CENTER SKULL ON
HIS CHEST—
(THE T-SHIRT SKULL,
NOT BUFORD'S SKULL)

Baljeet Rai

Baljeet is a mathematics and science whiz who values education above all else. (Hooray, school!) He is extremely intelligent, but more than a little sheltered. Once he's able to move past his insatiable need for schedules and grades, he can have as much fun as anyone.

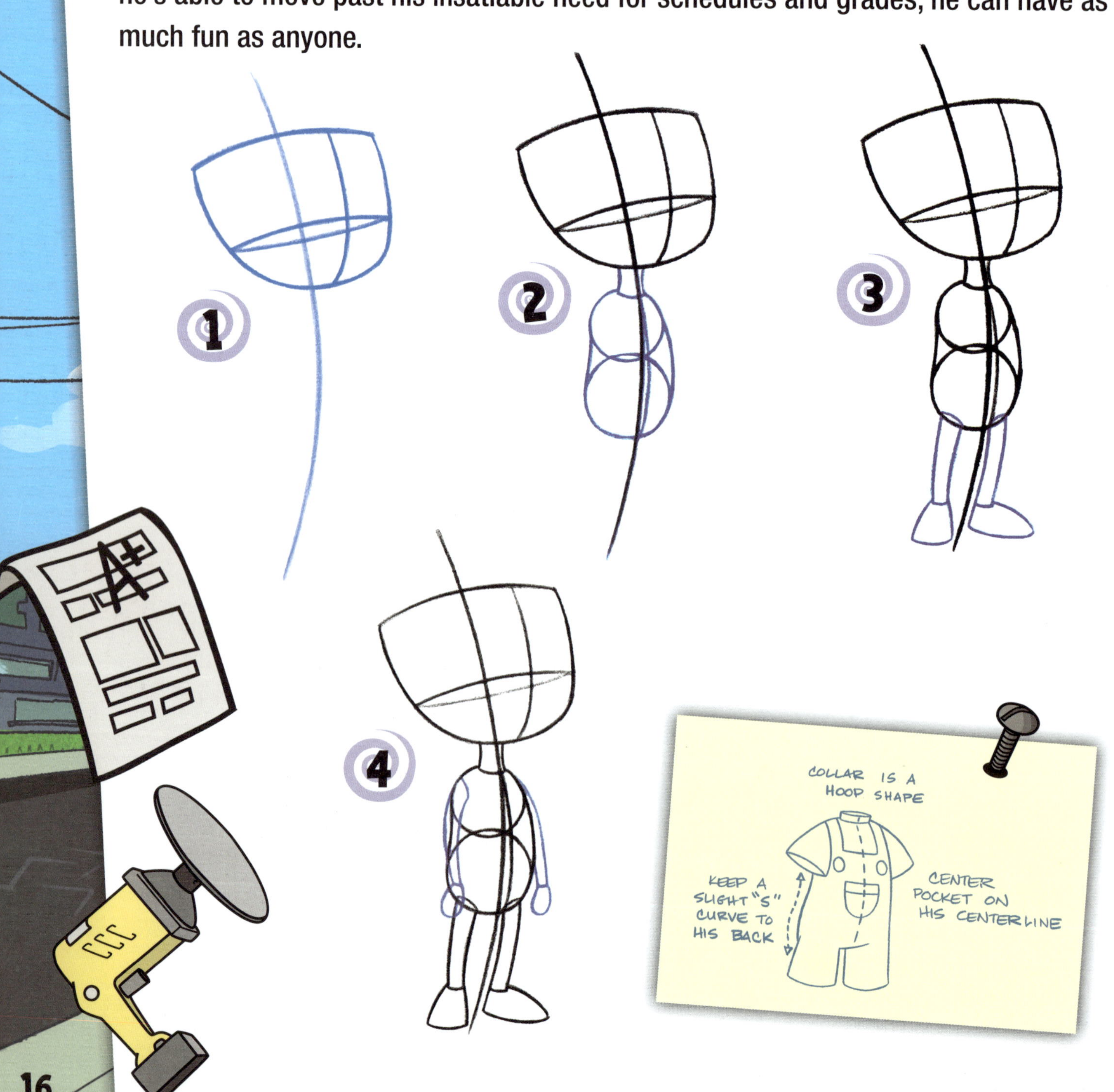

5
6
EYEBROWS ARE ON A CURVE
BACK OF HEAD HAS A SHARP EDGE LIKE HIS SLIDE RULE
USE "3" EAR DETAIL
7
8

Jeremy Johnson

Jeremy is Candace's even-tempered crush. He can usually be found working at Slushee Dawg; teaching guitar lessons; or playing with his band, Jeremy and the Incidentals. He is very calm and unflappable…in direct contrast to Candace.

5
8

6

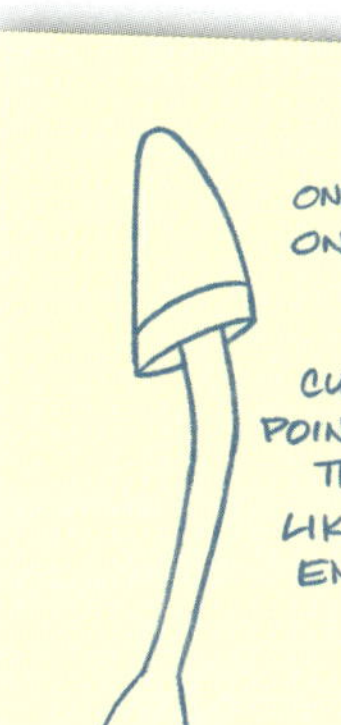
ONE STRIPE ON SLEEVE
CUFFS HAVE POINTS TO THEM – LIKE AN ENVELOPE
HANDS HAVE ANATOMY AND STRUCTURE, BUT NO FIFTH FINGER – GO FIGURE

7

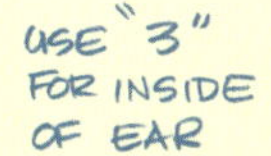
JEREMY HAS 3 LOCKS OF HAIR
USE "3" FOR INSIDE OF EAR
HIS MOUTH IS ALWAYS PLACED OFF TO THE SIDE CLOSEST TO VIEWER
COLLAR IS A RING SHAPE – IT IS NOT FLAT

Isabella Garcia-Shapiro

Isabella is the courageous, confident young lady who always greets her friends with a peppy, "Whatcha doin'?" As leader of the Fireside Girls, she is always prepared, resourceful, and ready to help—especially if it's Phineas who needs the help!

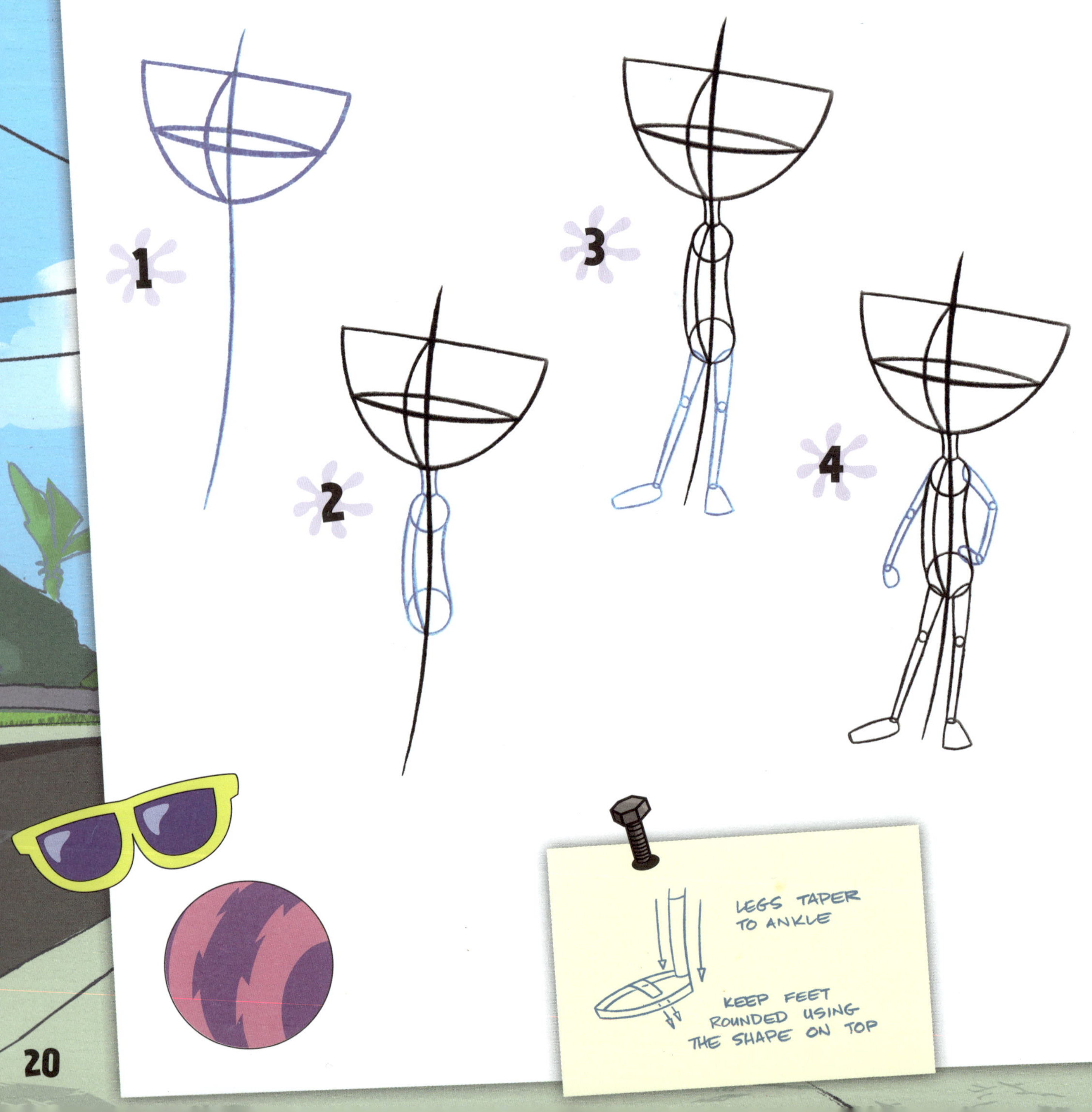

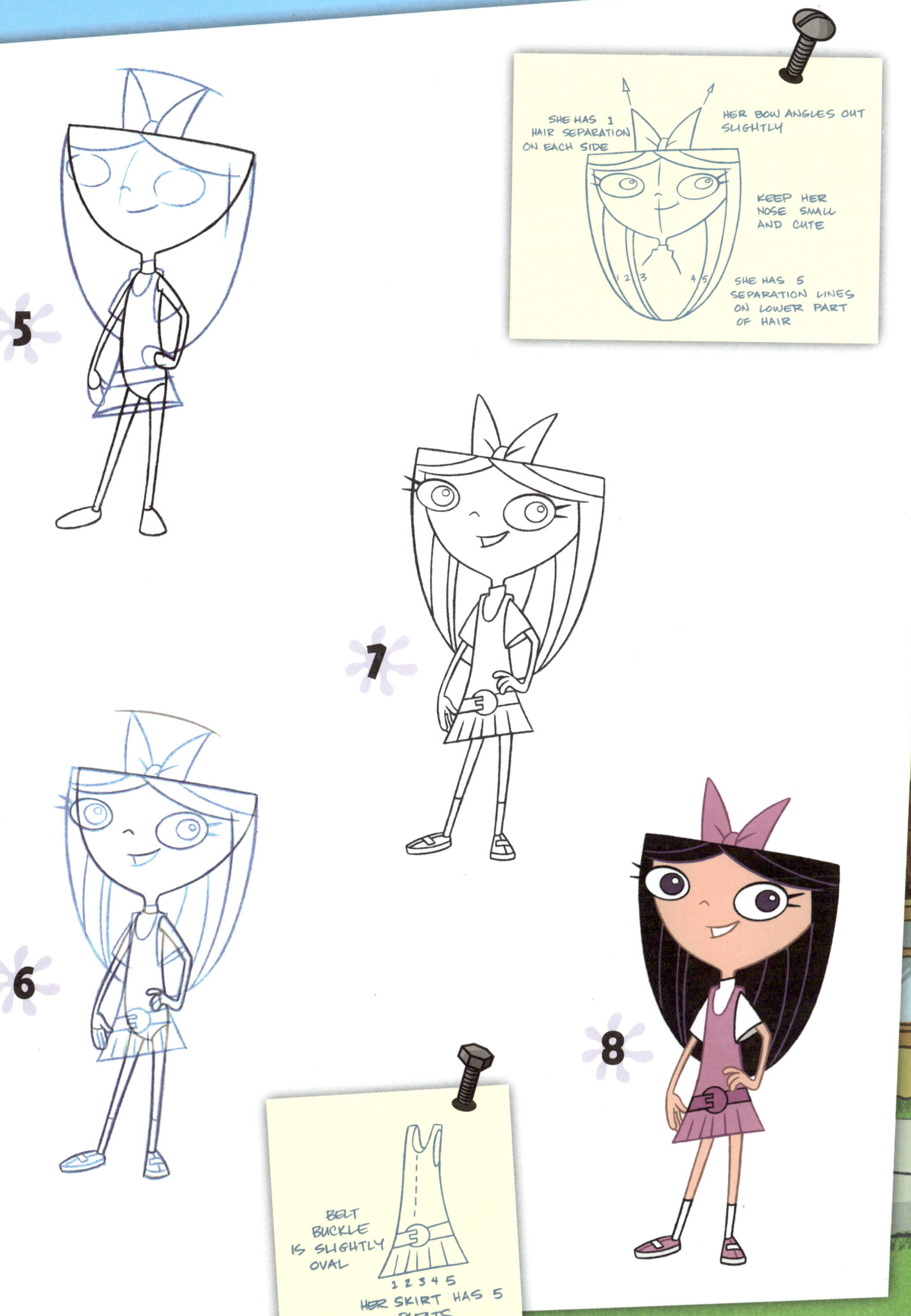
SHE HAS 1 HAIR SEPARATION ON EACH SIDE
HER BOW ANGLES OUT SLIGHTLY
KEEP HER NOSE SMALL AND CUTE
1 2 3
4 5
SHE HAS 5 SEPARATION LINES ON LOWER PART OF HAIR
5
7
6
8
BELT BUCKLE IS SLIGHTLY OVAL
1 2 3 4 5
HER SKIRT HAS 5 PLEATS

Perry the Platypus

Perry is the Flynn-Fletcher family's beloved pet: a web-footed, egg-laying, semi-aquatic mammal who doesn't do much when the family is around. He likes to sit under a tree, sleep on the boys' beds, and occasionally make an odd platypus sound. Oh, and he's also known as a secret agent called Agent P.

5
6
7
8
3 HAIRS ARE CENTERED ON HEAD WITH THE LONGEST IN THE MIDDLE
EYES SHOULD BE A BIT OFF KILTER
BILL HAS MASS AND TAPERS TO FACE
FRONT LEGS CURVE IN
IT HELPS TO LINE UP 3 DIAMONDS ON THE CENTER LINE
1 2 3 4 5
1 2 3 4
THE TAIL HAS THICKNESS- IT IS NOT FLAT
HIS HIND END IS FLAT AND HIS TAIL CAN ROTATE, WHICH IS BETTER THAN THE OTHER WAY AROUND

Agent P

Agent P is a secret agent of OWCA, operating from a hidden lair beneath Phineas and Ferb's house. He is brave, clever, and a master of platyjitsu, often using his tail as a lethal weapon against his nemesis, Dr. Doofenshmirtz.

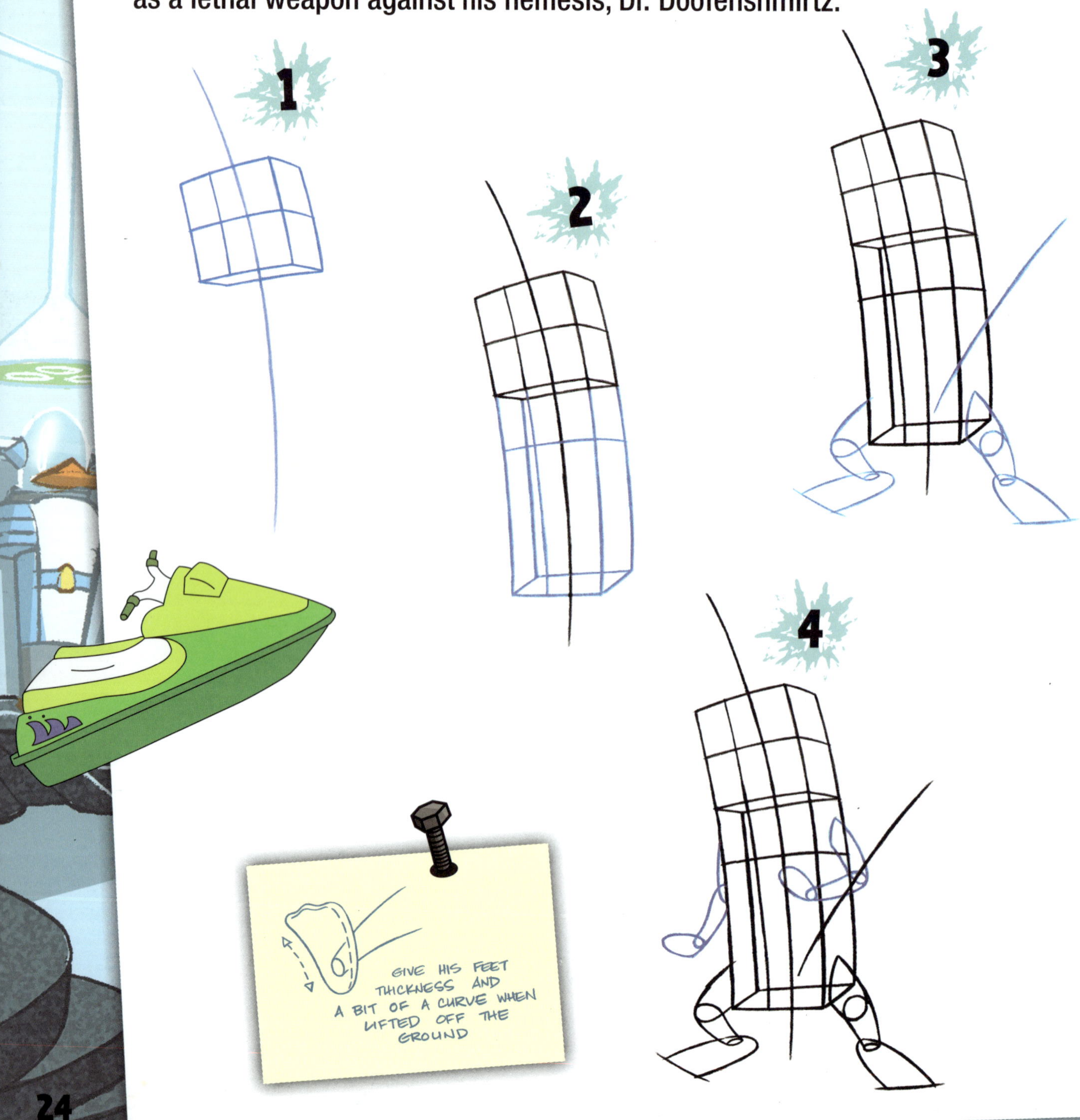

5
6
7
HE USUALLY HAS A DETERMINED EXPRESSION
HIS HAIR IS CENTERED ON HIS BOX-SHAPED HEAD
8
AGENT P IS MADE UP OF CURVES (DESPITE HAVING NERVES OF STEEL!)
TRI STATE

Linda Flynn-Fletcher

Linda is a busy mom who does more errands in one day than most people do in a month. She was once a pop star known as Lindana, but now she plays smooth jazz at the Squat N' Stitch. Her patience and dry sense of humor help her deal with Candace's constant interruptions.

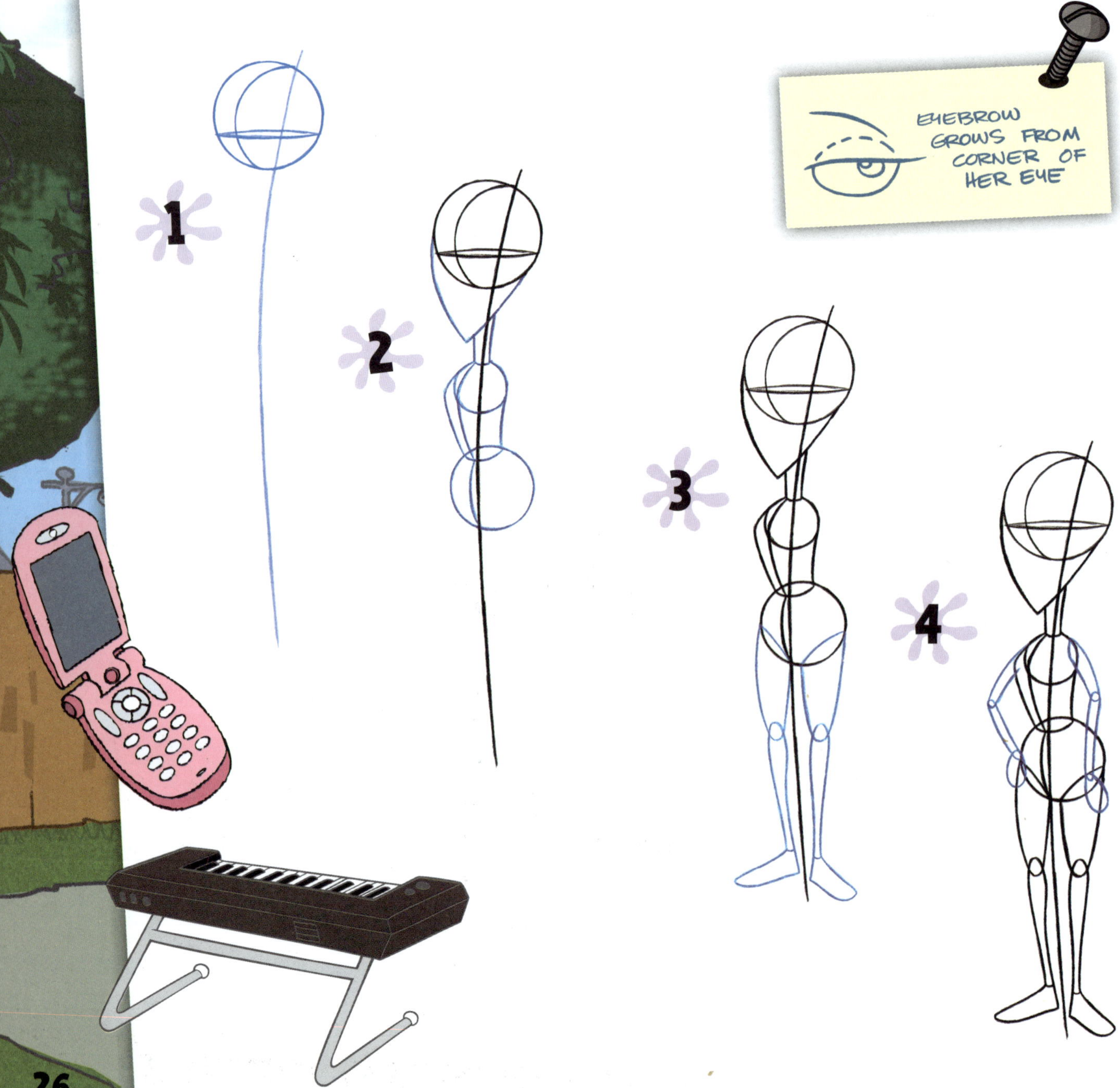

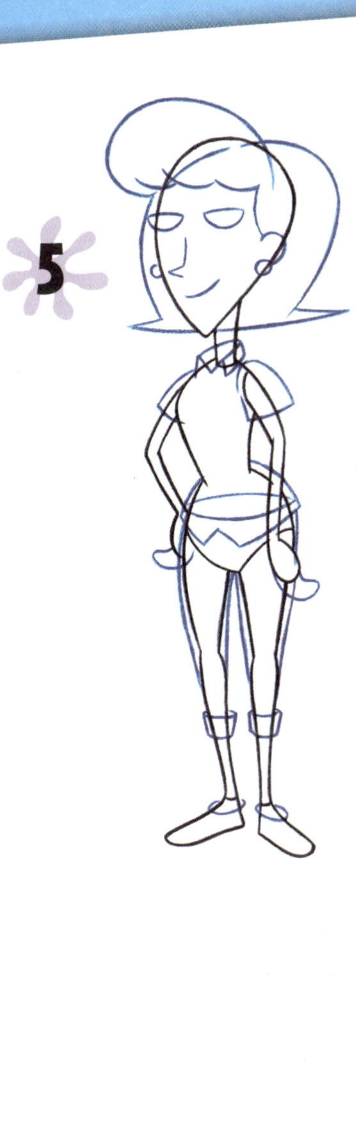
5

6

4 CLUMPS
OF HAIR
1 2 3 4
MOUTH
GOES TO SIDE
CLOSEST TO
VIEWER
"3" IN
EAR
KEEP HER
NECK CURVED
ARMS ARE
LOW ON TORSO

7

8

TAPER LEG
DOWN TO
ANKLE
CUFF IS
LARGER IN
FRONT
NO SOCKS!

Lawrence Fletcher

Lawrence, Phineas and Ferb's dad, hails from jolly old England. He runs an antique store in Danville, and he tells bad jokes. He is vaguely aware that his sons take on some major projects, which he thinks are "brilliant," in the most English sense of the word.

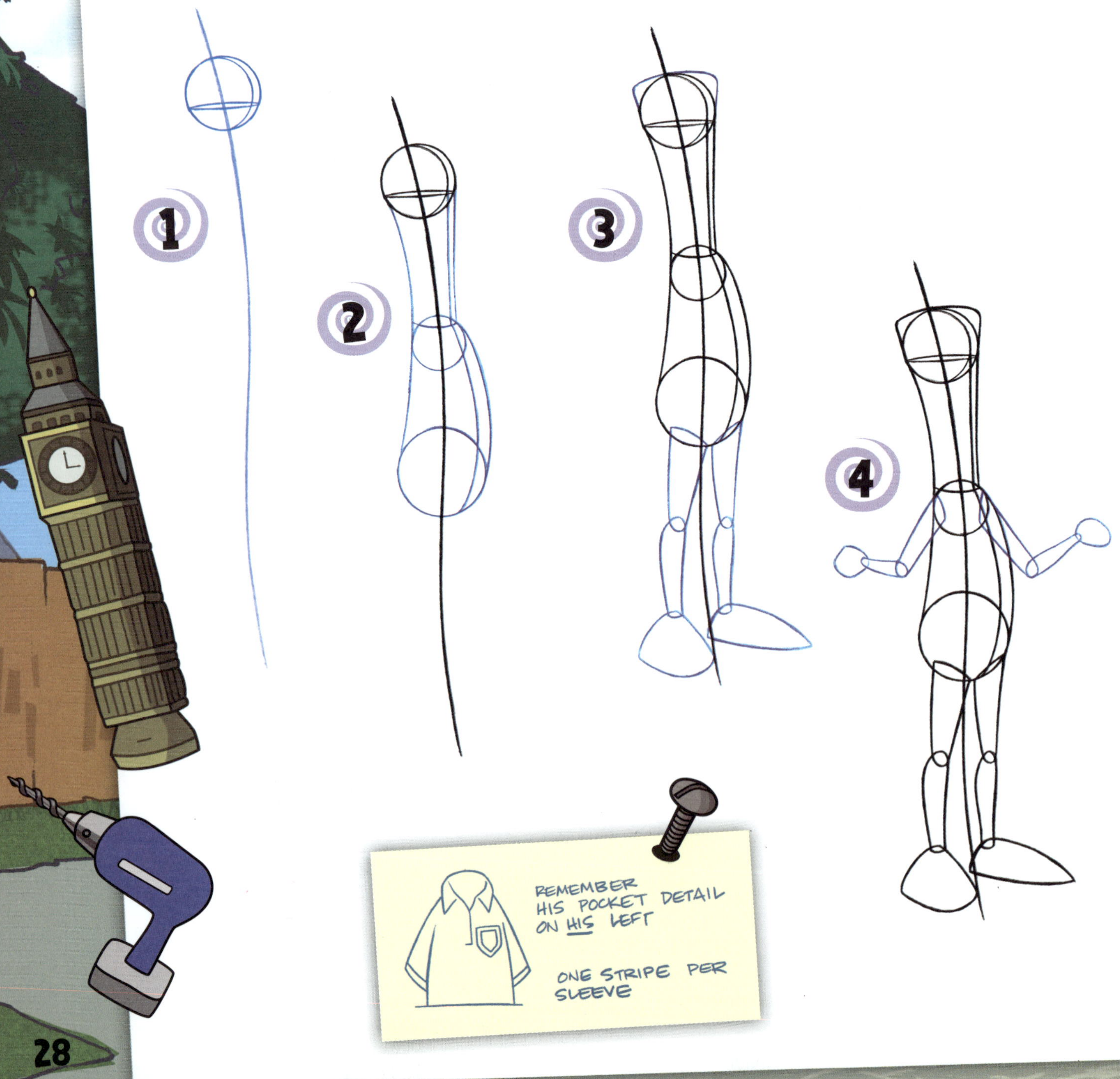

5
6
7
8
DAD HAS
3 LOCKS OF HAIR
1
2
3
FROM THIS
SIDE THE
"3" IS
BACKWARD
HE HAS A
NOTCH ON
HIS GLASSES
BETWEEN
EYES
HIS LIPS
JUT OUT
SLIGHTLY
DAD HAS NO CHIN
SORRY, MOM
DON'T LET
HIS NOSE GET
TOO SHARP
KEEP
HIS FEET
ROUND USING
SHOE DETAIL

Dr. Heinz Doofenshmirtz

Doof is driven. He is tenacious. He is a talented inventor. If Agent P didn't show up to defeat him, he'd find a way to defeat himself. But despite constant failures, he will never give up on his dream to rule the entire Tri-State Area!

5
6
7
8
HE OFTEN
STANDS WITH
KNEES BENT
DOOF HAS
6 LOCKS OF
HAIR
1
2
3
4
5
6
HE HAS
DARK CIRCLES
UNDER HIS
EYES
TEETH ARE
LARGE AND
OFF KILTER
"3"
IN EAR
COLLAR IS
A RING - NOT
FLAT

Vanessa Doofenshmirtz

Vanessa is the cool daughter of Dr. Heinz Doofenshmirtz. She's a laid-back teen who dresses in all black and is rarely emotional except when her father mortifies her with his embarrassing antics. She knows he means well, but he's still a big doof.